REFUGEES

© Aladdin Books Ltd 1990

First published in 1990
in the United States by
Gloucester Press
387 Park Avenue South
New York NY 10016

Design: Rob Hillier, Andy Wilkinson
Editor: Jen Green
Picture researcher: Cecilia Weston-Baker
Illustrator: Trev Lawrence

Library of Congress Cataloging-in-Publication Data
Hitchcox, Linda
    Refugees / Linda Hitchcox.
        p. cm. -- (Issues)
    Summary: Examines the status of refugees, their plight
and hardships, and discusses international efforts to help and
the difficult problems of asylum.
    ISBN 0-531-17242-2
    1. Refugees--Juvenile literature. 2. Asylum. Right of--
Juvenile literature. [1. Refugees.] I. Title.
    JV6346.R4H58   1990
    325'.21--dc20   90-3230   CIP   AC

Printed In Belgium

Front cover: Vietnamese boat people in Hong Kong in 1989.
Back cover: East Germans arrive in Nuremberg, 1989.

The author, Dr. Linda Hitchcox, is a social anthropologist attached to
the Institute of Social Anthropology, Oxford University. She has been
engaged in research on forced migration since 1985.

The consultant, Jill Rutter, is Education Officer for The Refugee
Council.

Contents

REFUGEES

LINDA HITCHCOX

Gloucester Press

New York : London : Toronto : Sydney

The refugee crisis

In the world today, there are now more than 14 million people who are officially recognized as being refugees. There are many millions more who have been forced to leave their homes because of drought, famine, war, and persecution, and seek refuge in other countries.

We are faced with an enormous crisis which is causing widespread suffering and hardship. Almost every day, the media brings us news of conflict and of mass movements of people. They flee for their lives in regions of the world such as Central America, the Horn of Africa, and Central and Southeast Asia.

▽ Ethiopian refugees flee civil war and famine in their country, moving to the Sudan. In 1984-85 more than 300,000 moved; today there are more than 700,000 in the Sudan. At the same time, because of war in southern Sudan, there are movements of Sudanese to Ethiopia. Many die before aid becomes available.

Wherever they are from, most refugees urgently need help before they can establish a new life for themselves again. They have left everything behind — their homes, friends, families, jobs and belongings — and often have to face a totally strange environment, a different society and a different language. Many have suffered other kinds of trauma, such as imprisonment and torture, the death of loved ones, and near starvation themselves, either before they escaped or on the journey.

The scale of human misery in the refugee crisis poses an enormous challenge and raises many more important issues. What are some of the causes of refugee movement around the world? How do governments decide who is a refugee? Should this decision affect who gets help? What are the solutions to the refugee crisis?

Drought, famine and war are the commonest causes of refugee movements. A harsh infertile environment, where people just manage to support themselves, may become intolerable when war breaks out. Many people have no choice but to seek help elsewhere, usually in equally poor countries. This has been the situation in the Horn of Africa for many years.

Who is a refugee?

Deciding who is a refugee is complicated. Refugees are legally defined in the United Nations Convention of 1951 and Protocol of 1967. The convention defines a refugee as someone who leaves or is unable to return to their own country "owing to a well founded fear of being persecuted for reasons of race, religion, nationality, membership of a particular social group, or political opinion." The refugee must prove that he or she has been individually persecuted. But the Organization of African Unity (OAU) recognizes that many people are unable to prove that they have been personally threatened.

A refugee, defined by the OAU, is one who "owing to external aggression, occupation, foreign domination or events seriously disturbing public order... is compelled to leave his or her place of residence."

▽ Nearly six million refugees have left Afghanistan since the Soviet invasion in 1979.

People who arrive in another country trying to claim refugee status are usually referred to as *asylum seekers*. In developed countries it is becoming increasingly difficult to gain admission. Proving persecution can be a difficult and lengthy business and meanwhile the applicant has to wait, subject to restrictions or even detention.

While waiting, asylum seekers normally have guaranteed protection against being sent home, but if they are found not to have acceptable reasons for leaving their homeland, they are very likely to be sent back.

Some people resettle in another country as *quota* or *program* refugees, admitted according to their nationality when the governments of resettlement countries decide there are reasons to admit mass exoduses of people.

▽ Vietnamese boat people reach Hong Kong to seek asylum in June 1989.

Flight and reception

When refugees reach their first place of asylum, the welcome they receive there can vary a great deal. The majority come from impoverished countries in the Third World and are received by equally poor countries. They may join friends and relatives living across the border and settle down once more to earn a living and raise their own families.

Others go to refugee camps where they rely on official aid, which is often channeled through the United Nations High Commissioner for Refugees (UNHCR). There are many types of camps, from almost self-supporting settlements such as in Tanzania, to closed and tightly restricted detention centers like those in Hong Kong.

▽ Refugees from Eritrea province in Ethiopia flee civil war and drought. Many internally displaced refugees in Ethiopia have suffered from the government's "villagization scheme" which aims to concentrate scattered farmers into more easily controlled collectives.

▽ Tamil refugees seek asylum in local communities in southern India. In closed camps, however, it is common for refugees to be made to feel inferior. They rarely have influence over how the camp is run, or how their lives are organized.

In camps many refugees begin to feel they must rely on their helpers and may lose confidence. Refugees are usually resourceful, highly motivated people. They need help so that they can be self-sufficient as soon as possible, not made to feel that they are so helpless they have to depend on others to make decisions for them.

The United Nations and OAU definitions of refugees exclude many people forced to flee. This includes internal refugees, who have not left their country, but have gone to another region because of conflict. Others flee because of environmental crisis, a problem in many regions of the world. People who are forced to move because of a catastrophe, such as an earthquake, flood, drought or famine, are not normally officially regarded as refugees. Those who are moved to make way for a large development project, such as the building of a dam or forest clearance, may also not receive any help.

Political turmoil in Africa

Since the end of World War II, the countries of Africa have frequently been in a state of turmoil. There have been wars of revolution and liberation, such as in Algeria and Western Sahara, wars between states, and also economic and environmental crises. All these situations produce refugees.

One important cause of unrest is nationalism. This is the name given to the activities of a group of people with a distinct identity or outlook, who seek to establish their own government. The problem is that few of the national groups in Africa are united enough to form one independent modern state. Usually they are spread over several states, the majority in one and the minority in another, because of the way that Africa was divided when occupied by European countries in the 19th century (under colonialism). Nationalism often leads to conflict.

▷ Refugee movements in Africa in the 1980s.

▽ Apartheid, the political system operated in South Africa whereby the white minority oppress the black majority by denying them political power, also produces many refugees. Thousands of blacks have been forcibly moved to areas known as Bantustans, where living standards are poor. The injustice of this situation creates a great deal of tension and conflict, not just in South Africa, but in neighboring countries like Botswana, Mozambique, Namibia, and Zimbabwe. Below: ruins of Crossroads shanty town, burnt by "white caps."

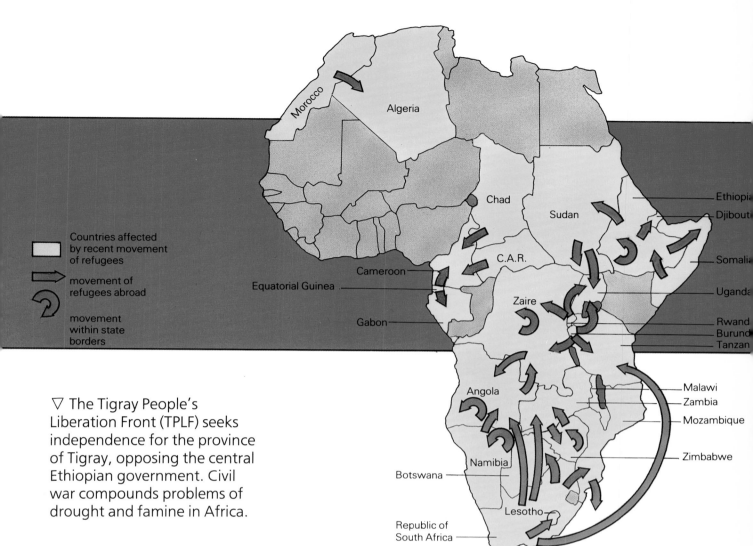

Countries affected
by recent movement
of refugees

movement of
refugees abroad

movement
within state
borders

Morocco
Algeria
Chad
Sudan
Ethiopia
Djibouti
C.A.R.
Cameroon
Equatorial Guinea
Somalia
Uganda
Zaire
Gabon
Rwanda
Burundi
Tanzania
Angola
Malawi
Zambia
Mozambique
Namibia
Zimbabwe
Botswana
Lesotho
Republic of
South Africa

▽ The Tigray People's
Liberation Front (TPLF) seeks
independence for the province
of Tigray, opposing the central
Ethiopian government. Civil
war compounds problems of
drought and famine in Africa.

In Sudan, Somalia and Ethiopia, the problems
of civil war and invasion have been worsened by
devastating famines and drought. These
countries host each other's refugees; by 1988
there were more than 800,000 Ethiopian refugees
in Somalia who had fled there in search of safety
and food. At the same time, Ethiopia was giving
asylum to 500,000 Somali refugees.

Solutions to the refugee crisis in Africa are
difficult to find. New movements of people begin
as others finish. The positive side of all these
tensions is the readiness of African people to
help each other. Few African refugees find
asylum in Europe. Instead, some of the poorest
countries in Africa receive and care for more than
4.5 million refugees who have fled from
neighboring governments.

Crisis in the Middle East and . . .

The Middle East has been constantly torn apart by conflict since the end of World War II. Refugees from Afghanistan form the largest single group of refugees in the world. More than three million live in Pakistan and about 2.8 million are in Iran. Most fled in 1979 when the Soviet Union invaded their country in support of the pro-Soviet republican government in Afghanistan. Many feared that their Islamic religion and way of life would be threatened, and many others left to avoid the fighting and destruction. Some returned later to join the resistance against the Soviet Army. Although the Soviet Union withdrew its troops from Afghanistan in 1989, the same government has held onto power and fighting continues between rival groups of Afghan people. Meanwhile millions of families wait on the borders of Afghanistan until it is safe to go home.

▷ Recent movements of Palestinian refugees.

▽ An Israeli soldier questions a Palestinian. One of the most enduring problems in the Middle East is the dilemma of the Palestinians. In 1948 the State of Israel was established. As Jewish refugees, many of whom had been persecuted under the Nazis, began arriving in Israel, 750,000 Palestinians were forced to leave their homes. They were promised a state of their own, but instead wait in refugee camps, many within territories occupied by Israel. Their protests have become increasingly violent and will lead to conflict unless a political solution is found.

West Asia

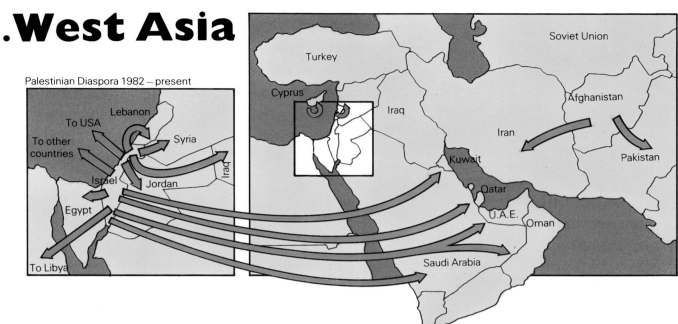

Palestinian Diaspora 1982 – present

Another distressed and dislocated group in this region is the 20 million Kurds who live as minorities in an arc from Iran west to Iraq and Turkey. They face torture and death for their wish to have a separate homeland. In 1988, several thousand Kurds were driven from their homes in northern Iraq by chemical weapons (banned by international agreements).

▽ More than two million Kurds have fled to Turkey, to face freezing conditions in tents during the winter. At Cukurca just inside the Turkish border, refugee Kurds living unsheltered try to get some warmth after a cold night.

Religious strife in South Asia

After World War II, India became independent from Britain. The disputes that arose between Hindus and Moslems were meant to be resolved with the partition of India in 1947. The new state of Pakistan was set up and eight million Moslems moved there from India. At the same time, six million Hindus fled with their belongings in the opposite direction. When the state of Bangladesh, previously part of Pakistan, emerged in 1971, millions more were displaced in the conflicts. Strife still continues between Moslems and Hindus in northern India.

The Indian state of Kashmir, which is mainly Moslem, has continually been a matter of disagreement between India and Pakistan. India accuses Moslem Pakistan of stirring up troubles aimed at bringing Kashmir into Pakistan.

▽ 14 million Hindus and Moslems fled after partition.

▷ Refugee movements in South Asia after 1970.

Soviet Union
China
Iran
Afghanistan
Tibet
Bhutan
Pakistan
Nepal
B
India
Bangladesh
Sri Lanka

△ In Lower Chusot, India, villagers carry a pot of tukpo soup to feed Tibetan children. North of India, in the Himalayan country of Tibet, countless Tibetans have suffered and fled the rule of communist China after the Chinese invasion in 1959. Nearly 90,000 Tibetans followed their leader, the Dalai Lama, into exile. Those who remained in Tibet suffered persecution as the Chinese made every effort to stamp out Tibetan language and culture. Most refugee Tibetans were given asylum in India. There they have set up their own villages, schools and businesses. Their goal is to preserve and strengthen Tibetan culture until they can return to their homeland.

South of India, Sri Lanka forms another region of conflict. Sri Lanka (formerly Ceylon) gained independence in 1948 when the British left India. Political parties have since fought over power in a very unstable situation, partly created by the growing poverty of the country. The instability is also caused by the deep conflicts between the majority of the population who are Sinhalese and the minority group of Tamil people, who live mainly in the north of the country.

In 1983, bands of Sinhalese went on the rampage in Colombo, the capital city, making more than 250,000 people homeless. Many Tamils have sought safety abroad, mainly in the state of Tamil Nadu in southern India where more than 130,000 refugees now live. Approximately 5,000 others have fled to Europe and have found homes, particularly in France and Germany. Of the 5,000 people seeking asylum in Britain, only 33 had been granted full refugee status by April 1989. Despite widespread understanding that there is armed conflict in Sri Lanka, Tamils are still very likely to be labeled as economic migrants who have no right to enter the country.

Boat people of Southeast Asia

War and invasion in Southeast Asia, particularly Indochina, have resulted in widespread devastation, migration, and death. Vietnam has been the source of a large movement of refugees. Since communist North Vietnam defeated South Vietnam, nearly one million people have left the country, the first 130,000 with the help of American forces stationed there during the Vietnam War. Since then, refugees have left in small leaky boats, or traveled overland to Thailand and China. It has been estimated that as many as 60 percent do not survive the journey. Many thousands have died at sea, sometimes at the hands of pirates. When they reach asylum it may take up to two years for them to be assessed.

After perilous escapes from their own country, Vietnamese asylum seekers are held in closed detention centers in some countries until their cases are assessed. Closed camps like Hei Ling Chau in Hong Kong are overcrowded and there are no trees or grass.

▽ Vietnamese asylum seekers in Hong Kong live in nissen huts surrounded by concrete and barbed wire fences.

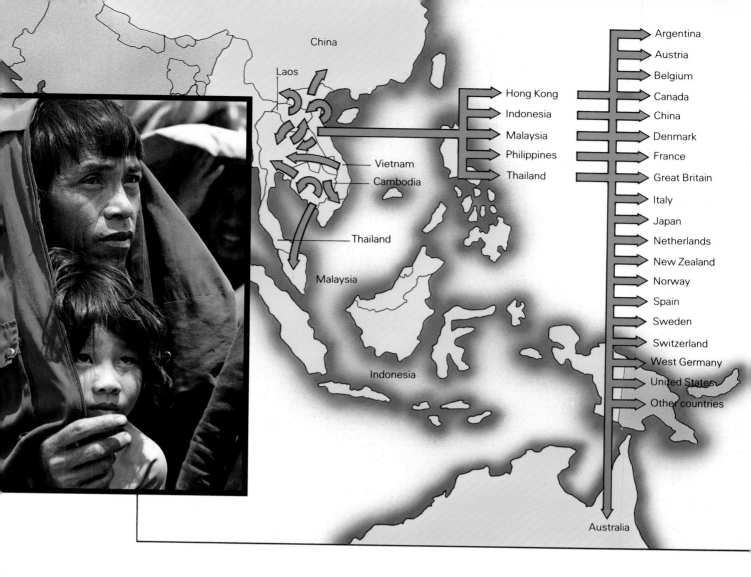

Refugee movements in Southeast Asia since 1975. Nearly every country in the region has provided a place of first asylum and from there, three-quarters of a million Vietnamese have been resettled elsewhere, mostly in the United States, Canada and in Australia.

Now countries are no longer so willing to resettle Vietnamese and screening procedures have been introduced to decide whether the applicant is genuine. If not, he or she will probably be returned to Vietnam.

In 1975, the communist Khmer Rouge took control of Cambodia and began a reign of terror. Most of the townspeople were forcibly sent to the countryside. More than one million people died in labor and torture camps; 150,000 refugees fled to Vietnam. They returned when Vietnam invaded in 1978. After Vietnam seized control of the country hundreds of thousands of frightened people, including Khmer Rouge supporters, escaped across the border to Thailand. There, camps were set up to receive the displaced people and they were given widespread international support. The 350,000 refugees on the border are involved in a guerrilla war against the Vietnamese-backed government. In 1989 the Vietnamese withdrew, leaving the government to fight on alone.

Rivalries in Latin America

Over the past ten years Central America has become known as a place of violent political change with mass deportations and widespread terrorist activities, particularly in El Salvador, Nicaragua and Guatemala. Probably more than two million people have been displaced, mostly women and children from rural areas. Camps have been set up in asylum countries such as Honduras and Mexico, but refugees will also settle among friends in the local population. As in Africa, the poorest nations in the world shelter many thousands of people.

In El Salvador, the war between the American backed military government and the left-wing opposition forces has caused the deaths of more than 50,000, and it is estimated that nearly 500,000 Salvadoreans have fled. Those who reached the United States were classified as illegal immigrants and therefore deported. More than 250,000 refugees left Nicaragua while the left-wing Sandinistas were in power.

After the coup in Chile in 1973, nearly one million people fled the severe repression and violence. The release of political prisoners was sometimes obtained by arranging for them to go into exile. In some areas, sponsorships were found for them. In the Scandinavian countries where people are sympathetic to socialist politics, Chileans received a great welcome. In the United States, the refugees from Chile had a more difficult time. However, in the last few years, there has been a change of government and Chileans have been returning to their country.

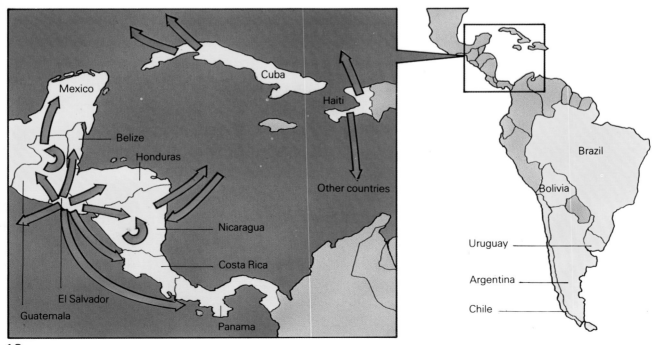

In Latin America between 1970 and 1976, military governments seized control in Bolivia, Uruguay, Chile and Argentina, and established repressive dictatorships. Thousands of people fled their countries. Many others suffered severe torture in prison. In Argentina, from 1976 to 1983 when the armed forces held power, 30,000 people were seized and never seen again. Others survived imprisonment and were later expelled. Many of these left Latin America altogether.

△ In 1980 the mothers and grandmothers of thousands of "the disappeared," victims of the tyranny in Argentina, held vigils in the Plaza de Mayo in Buenos Aires to protest against the government's brutal crimes. The publicity they attracted made it very difficult for the government to suppress them.

◁ Refugee hotspots in Latin America since 1970.

▷ A Contra soldier near the Nicaraguan border. Until February 1990 the Sandinista government in Nicaragua was fighting Contra guerrillas who until recently were funded by the United States. More than 50,000 people were displaced by the war, particularly Miskito Indians. In 1990 a coalition government replaced the Sandinistas, and some refugees are returning.

Reaching safety

When refugees flee their homes, their initial reaction is relief that they have escaped immediate danger, but the journey to a place of safety can be a very dangerous and traumatic enterprise. They will also realize that their home and all their possessions have been lost.

Most refugees remain in countries of first asylum. Sometimes they settle themselves on the land, merging in with the local population, either legally or illegally. This may be a satisfactory solution, as they do not experience the dependency which camp life can bring, and may quickly become part of the community.

Many governments, however, are unwilling to let refugees settle where they want. Most people end up in camps where they can be more easily administered. Many refugees wait for a long time before a permanent solution is found for them.

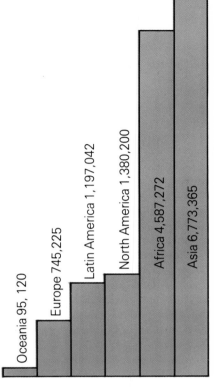

Oceania 95, 120

Europe 745,225

Latin America 1,197,042

North America 1,380,200

Africa 4,587,272

Asia 6,773,365

△ Nasir Bagh refugee camp near Peshawar in Pakistan. Afghan refugees began arriving in Pakistan on a massive scale in 1979 after the Soviet invasion. By 1986, the refugee population numbered about three million.

△ Figures of refugees received by continent. The poorest countries care for the vast majority of asylum seekers.

◁ Ethiopian refugees construct a shelter in Somalia. The refugees have been assisted by international aid which has included irrigation schemes and tree planting. Their need for construction materials (see left) and firewood soon threatens to cause widespread deforestation in this drought-stricken area. UNHCR has begun to assist people to return to Ethiopia.

Other refugee camps are placed close to borders and may be liable to border raids. The refugees may themselves be forcibly recruited into counterattacking guerrilla armies, as has happened on the Thai-Cambodian border or in the Salvadorean camps in Honduras. Refugee camps in occupied territories are very tightly restricted. In the Palestinian refugee camps in territories seized by Israel in 1967 , there is continual violence as Palestinians resist the Israeli security forces. Protection of refugees is the prime function of UNHCR, but it is not always possible to achieve, especially in remote regions in a state of turmoil.

Resettlement in the west

One long-term option for refugees is to move from the country where they first found asylum, and resettle in another country. Many refugees seek resettlement, because it is seen as a safe solution and may also provide opportunities of education and employment, which help to compensate for the new, strange and stressful environment. These countries are usually in the industrialized, developed world, particularly Europe and North America, which do not produce large numbers of refugees. But the arrival of many thousands of asylum seekers in Europe has caused governments to operate more restrictive asylum procedures in recent years.

The United States still has a large refugee program (94,000 in 1989), but continues to favor some nationalities when granting admission. In 1989 the majority of refugees came from Indochina and the Soviet Bloc (77,000). The government assistance program for refugees coming to America is designed to help refugees become self-sufficient as soon as possible.

△ Nobel prize-winning physicist Albert Einstein (1879-1955) was a Jewish refugee who left Germany in 1933 after the Nazis seized his house and burned his works. He never returned. Few refugees are allowed to resettle in the West, although they have often made a positive contribution to the societies they enter.

▽ As a result of the persecution of the Jews by the Nazis in Germany, 10,000 unaccompanied Jewish children came to Britain. It was an arrangement that saved their lives, but most of them never saw their parents again.

△ Author Alexander Solzhenitsyn was imprisoned from 1945 to 1953 and expelled from the Soviet Union in 1974 after the publication of *The Gulag Archipelago*.

Europe has resettled significant numbers of refugees, mainly from Eastern Europe, Indochina and South America. Many of these have come on arranged "quota" programs for mass movements of refugees.

The largest group living in the European Community is from Eastern Europe. Since the end of World War II, when the East European states came under the control of governments allied to the Soviet Union, there has been a steady movement of refugees escaping to the west. This situation changed dramatically in 1989, when the restrictions on freedom of movement were relaxed in Hungary, East Germany, and Czechoslovakia.

A refugee's nationality may affect the outcome of application for asylum. In Britain, Tamils and Kurds have been refused. In the United States, 2.7% of Salvadoreans were accepted in 1988, compared with 50% acceptance of other national groups such as Nicaraguans. In France, 86.7% of Europeans received asylum in 1987 compared to 9.4% of Africans.

▽ In 1989, thousands of East Germans flooded across the West German border.

Going home

Going home, or repatriation, is regarded as the ideal solution, because it is assumed that most refugees want to return to their homeland if at all possible. Many people wander back informally when they tire of enduring the hardships of the camps; others are flown or bussed back in special programs. The problem is that they rarely wish to return when the conditions from which they fled have not changed a great deal.

Attitudes toward refugees in developed countries have altered, a change popularly known as "compassion fatigue." Legislation in Europe has been tightened to keep asylum seekers out. New visa restrictions may prevent them leaving in the first place. Sometimes refugees are sent from one government to the next as each refuses to consider their case. In 1986, a group of Cambodian "refugees in orbit" flew from Bangkok to Munich to London back to Bangkok then to Kuala Lumpur, London and Paris, spending more than 60 hours in the air, before authorities at last agreed to help.

Developed countries have changed their attitudes to refugees for complex reasons. Populations have increased, land has grown more scarce and social problems have multiplied. Automation and technology have meant an end to the shortage of unskilled workers in industrial countries.

▽ Salvadorean refugees leave Colomoncagua camp in Honduras to return home. Refugees who fled from El Salvador to Honduras in 1981 because of civil war have now begun to go back. But there are difficulties in finding out what happens afterward. There have been equally mixed reports of repatriation programs in the Sudan, southern India, and Djibouti.

In 1989 the British and Hong Kong governments began negotiating with the government of Vietnam to return asylum seekers who had left Vietnam for Hong Kong. This group has been screened and officially classified as not being genuine refugees, but migrants. Consequently they are not being given the option of resettlement, but must return to Vietnam.

There is concern about what will happen when they are sent back to the regime they escaped. Monitoring the experiences of returnees is a very complicated exercise. In humanitarian terms, returning people against their will is a violation of the Declaration of Human Rights.

Statement of a Guatemalan woman who was being returned from Mexico: We escaped to Mexico because we didn't want to die. And we don't want to go back now. They say it is quiet now, but we are afraid of going back. Suddenly there will be violence again....The flesh is afraid of dying. Thanks to Mexico... we eat and sleep peacefully.

▽ Vietnamese asylum seekers protest in Hong Kong, 1989.

Refugee children

▽ At Dodba refugee camp in Pakistan these Afghan boys study in their own school. For many children the experience of flight was traumatic and harrowing. One Afghan child was five years old when he followed his mother through deep snow to the Pakistan border. He remembered crying from hunger, but what terrified him most of all was the thought that he was leaving his father behind in Afghanistan, perhaps forever.

More than one half of the world's refugee population are children. Often in situations of conflict it is the children who manage to escape, sometimes with horrific memories of soldiers who killed or imprisoned their parents. The journey is often frightening and dangerous. Sometimes parents deliberately remain behind to enable their children to leave safely.

In 1938, at the start of the persecution of the Jews by the Nazi regime, 10,000 unaccompanied children were allowed to go to Britain. Many never saw their parents again. Nowadays unaccompanied refugee children still arrive in Britain, often from Vietnam and the Horn of Africa. Once there they have many problems to face in getting used to the strange food, the strange customs of British people, making friends, settling into school and learning the new language. Remarkably, many of them cope well.

Other refugee children are not fortunate enough to be resettled, but remain in the refugee camps. Many are born there and grow up knowing no other life than the restricted routine of the camp. The young children do not know what it is like to go shopping, to have a family meal, to have their own home. The older ones remember their old lives and these memories add to their frustrations.

Refugee children are urgently in need of protection in the camps. They are vulnerable to malnutrition and disease, and also to every kind of abuse, when family and friends are not there to protect them. In camps on the Thai-Cambodian border, some impoverished families are reduced to selling or renting out their children for work such as carrying water. In conditions of extreme poverty, child abuse flourishes; often refugee camps are no exception.

There are more than 80 international statutes concerned with human rights for children. Many of these have been included in a Convention on the Rights of the Child. One section specifically deals with refugee children, their protection and assistance. Such children need this support if they are to cope with their nightmare experiences and develop fulfilling and meaningful lives.

▽ At Kumrao in India, Tibetan children enjoy the lighter side of their heritage.

What is being done?

UNHCR is the main agency responsible for the protection and assistance of refugees. It does not usually assist them directly, but instead cooperates with governments, voluntary agencies and other UN organizations. They provide the people who set up camps and kitchens, dig wells, provide medical care or arrange disaster relief in an emergency.

There are many voluntary organizations, mostly from the industrialized nations: Europe, the United States and Japan. Refugees also form their own support organizations and participate in relief programs. The developing nations contribute by providing land and resources for refugees, since these are generally the countries of first asylum. Many millions of dollars are spent on supporting refugees, yet still numbers grow.

▽ "Are we self-sufficient as refugees? What obstacles stand in our way?" reads the caption to this drawing by a Ugandan refugee boy in the Sudan. Refugees like the child from Ethiopia below need to recover from the physical and psychological trauma of their escape. They need to feel safe, and they also often want help in finding a place of settlement where they can stay either permanently or until they can return to their old homes. After that, it is important for them to feel that they can take charge of their own lives and be independent as much as possible.

By AƆRANYA ISS KALA SE

△ Famine relief in the Sudan, provided by the International Committee of the Red Cross. Many voluntary organizations in the west help to organize assistance for refugees. It is beginning to be recognized that there must be international cooperation between governments of refugee-producing and refugee-receiving nations, to try and tackle the reasons why people have made the decision to leave.

Refugee facts

Refugee hotspots in the 1980s.

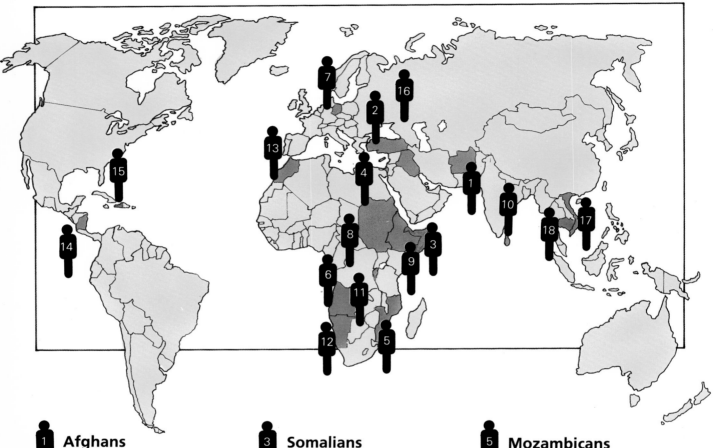

1 Afghans
6,000,000 Afghans have fled the civil war since the Soviet invasion in 1979. 3,500,000 live in camps in Pakistan, in increasingly unstable circumstances; 2,500,000 live in Iran among the local people.

2 Kurds
Kurds are a persecuted group living in the countries of Iran, Iraq and Turkey; 1,000,000 are refugees. Iraq has used chemical weapons against them. 4,000 Alevi Kurds from Turkey have fled persecution to Britain.

3 Somalians
Refugees of civil war, 600,000 Somalians endure near starvation in camps in Ethiopia, and more than 300,000 have been internally displaced. Famine is a grave problem in the region.

4 Palestinians
Of the 2,500,000 Palestinian refugees, nearly half live in restricted circumstances in the occupied territories seized by Israel in the Six Day War of 1967. Palestinians want their own homeland.

5 Mozambicans
More than 1,000,000 Mozambicans have fled to Malawi, Tanzania and Zambia to escape the atrocities of RENAMO, an insurgency group. 3,300,000 are internally displaced.

6 Angolans
Almost 550,000 Angolans have sought refuge from internal strife. Some 450,000 have fled to the towns for safety, and 97,000 have crossed the border, to Zambian camps with meager rations.

Germans

7 Since the border between West and East Germany was opened in 1989, 90,000 East Germans have moved to West Germany. Around 320,000 ethnic Germans have arrived from Poland, Romania and the USSR.

Sudanese

8 Of 2,000,000 Sudanese displaced by the civil war between the government and the People's Liberation Army, 350,000 have fled to Ethiopia, with thousands more arriving every month. Hundreds of thousands have died of starvation.

Ethiopians

9 1,100,000 Ethiopians have fled war in Tigray and Eritrea provinces to Somalia and Sudan, and more are internally displaced through the government's "villagization" program to concentrate farms.

Tamils

10 Over 100,000 Tamil refugees have fled civil war in their homeland of Sri Lanka to southern India, to Britain, and elsewhere, but they have had difficulty in claiming asylum and some have been forcibly returned to Sri Lanka.

Burundians and Rwandans

11 267,000 Rwandan and 60,000 Burundian refugees have crossed the borders between their two small countries fleeing the conflict between the Tutsi and Hutu peoples.

Namibians

12 Since the 1970s large numbers of Namibians have been displaced in the struggle for independence from South Africa. 42,000 went to Zambia and Angola. Independence was declared in March 1990.

Western Saharans

13 167,000 Sahrawi refugees have fled from this former Spanish colony since Morocco took control in 1975, traveling to harsh desert regions of Algeria where drinking water is very scarce.

Nicaraguans and Salvadoreans

14 More than 1,000,000 Salvadoreans and 50,000 Nicaraguans have fled civil war and are scattered throughout Central America. In 1990 a coalition government replaced the Sandinistas.

Haitians

15 More than 1,000,000 Haitians have fled military-style dictatorships and extreme poverty to countries including the United States, Dominican Republic, Canada and France.

Soviet Jews

16 Under Gorbachev's new liberalization policies, many thousands of Jews are able to leave the USSR, for Israel and the United States. Palestinian hopes of securing their own homeland are diminished by their arrival in Israel.

Vietnamese

17 Since unification of Vietnam in 1975, nearly 1,000,000 refugees have fled to first asylum countries in Southeast Asia, and from there to the west. Repatriation programs were set up in 1989.

Cambodians

18 Hundreds of thousands of Cambodians were internally displaced from 1975 to 1978 by the Khmer Rouge regime. 350,000 fled over the Thai border in 1978 when the Vietnamese invaded. The civil war continues.

31

Index

Photographic Credits
Cover and pages 8, 16, 19 top, 22 middle, 23, 29 and back cover: Frank Spooner; pages 4-5: S. Salgado/Magnum; pages 6, 7, 17, 25 and 28 right: Associated Press/Topham Picture Library; pages 8-9, 11 and 24: M. Goldwater/Network; page 10: Mendel/Magnum; page 12: C. Steele-Perkins/Magnum; pages 13 and 19 bottom: Nachtwey/Magnum; page 14: B. Barbey/Magnum; pages 15, 20 bottom, 22 bottom, 26 and 27: Save the Children Fund; page 20-21 top: McCurry/Magnum; page 22 top: Popperfoto; page 28 left: Author.